To those people who
believed in me, when I
could not.

"Here's to the crazy ones, the misfits, the rebels, the troublemakers, the round pegs in the square holes... the ones who see things differently -- they're not fond of rules... You can quote them, disagree with them, glorify or vilify them, but the only thing you can't do is ignore them because they change things... they push the human race forward, and while some may see them as the crazy ones, we see genius, because the ones who are crazy enough to think that they can change the world, are the ones who do."

– Steve Jobs

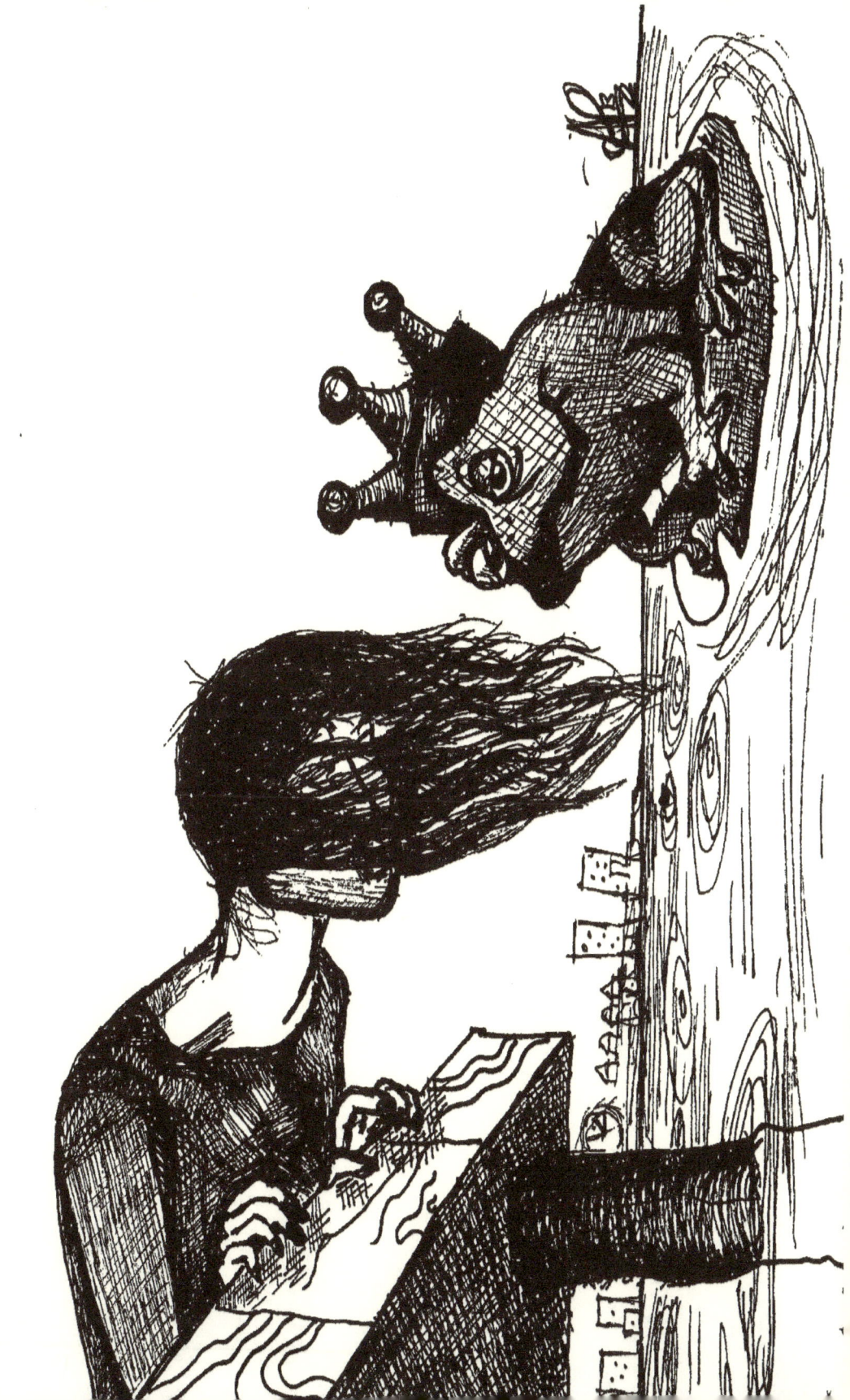

"Ah, Women. They make the highs higher and the lows more frequent."

– Friedrich Nietzsche

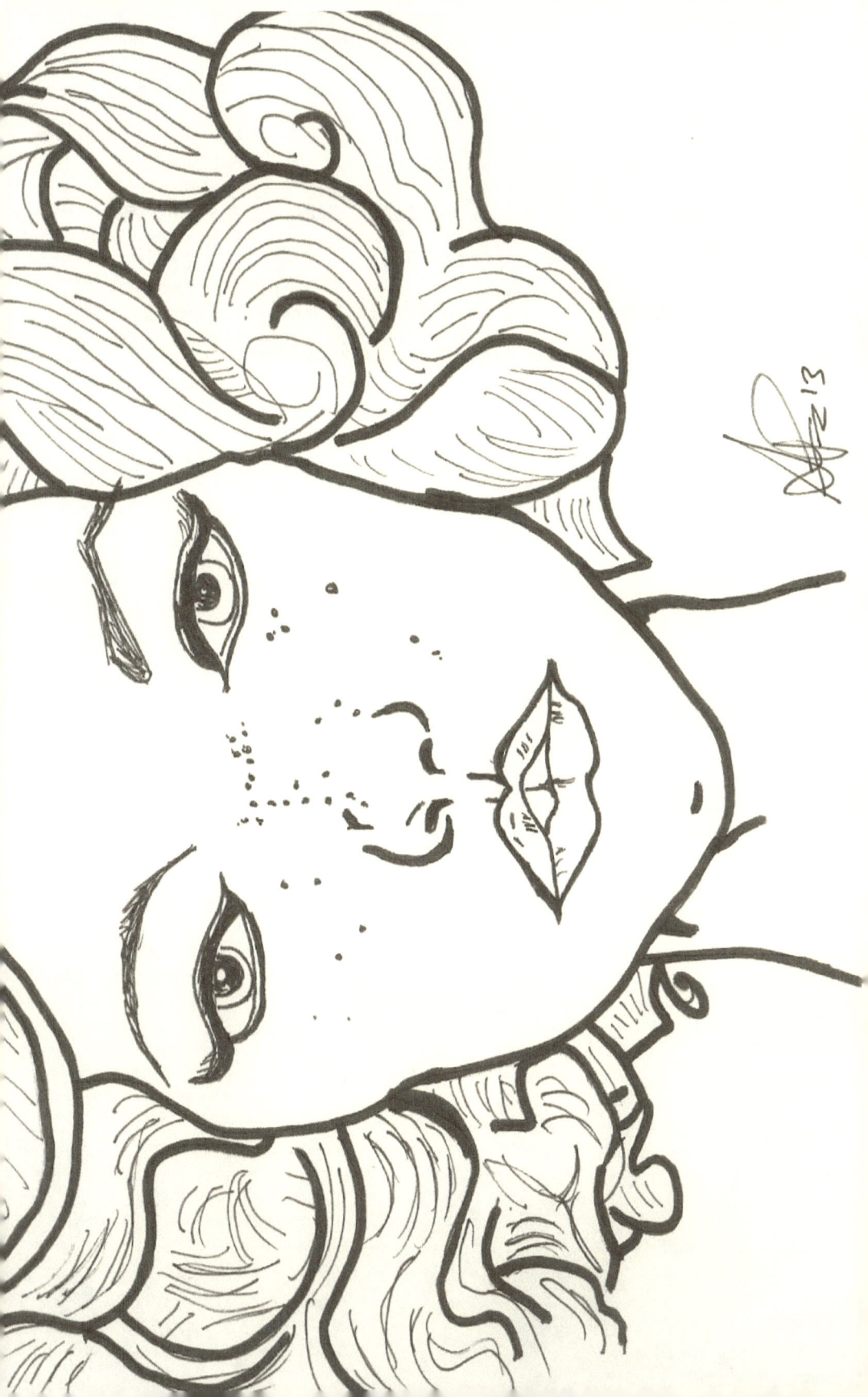

"Remember, sex is like a Chinese dinner. It ain't over 'til you both get your cookie."

- Alex Baldwin

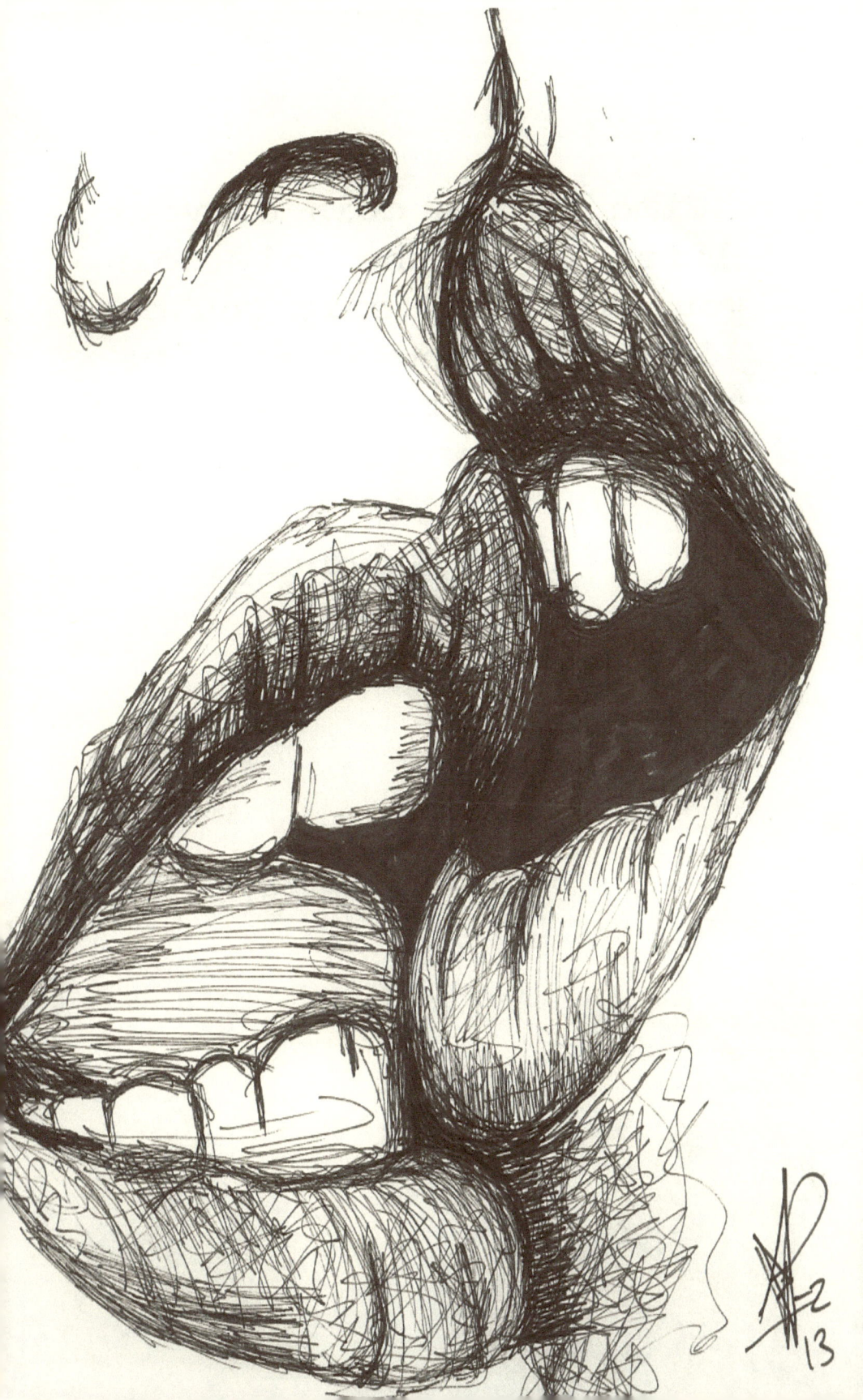

"Time is the coin of your life. It is the only coin you have, and only you can determine how it will be spent. Be careful lest you let other people spend it for you."

\- Carl Sandburg

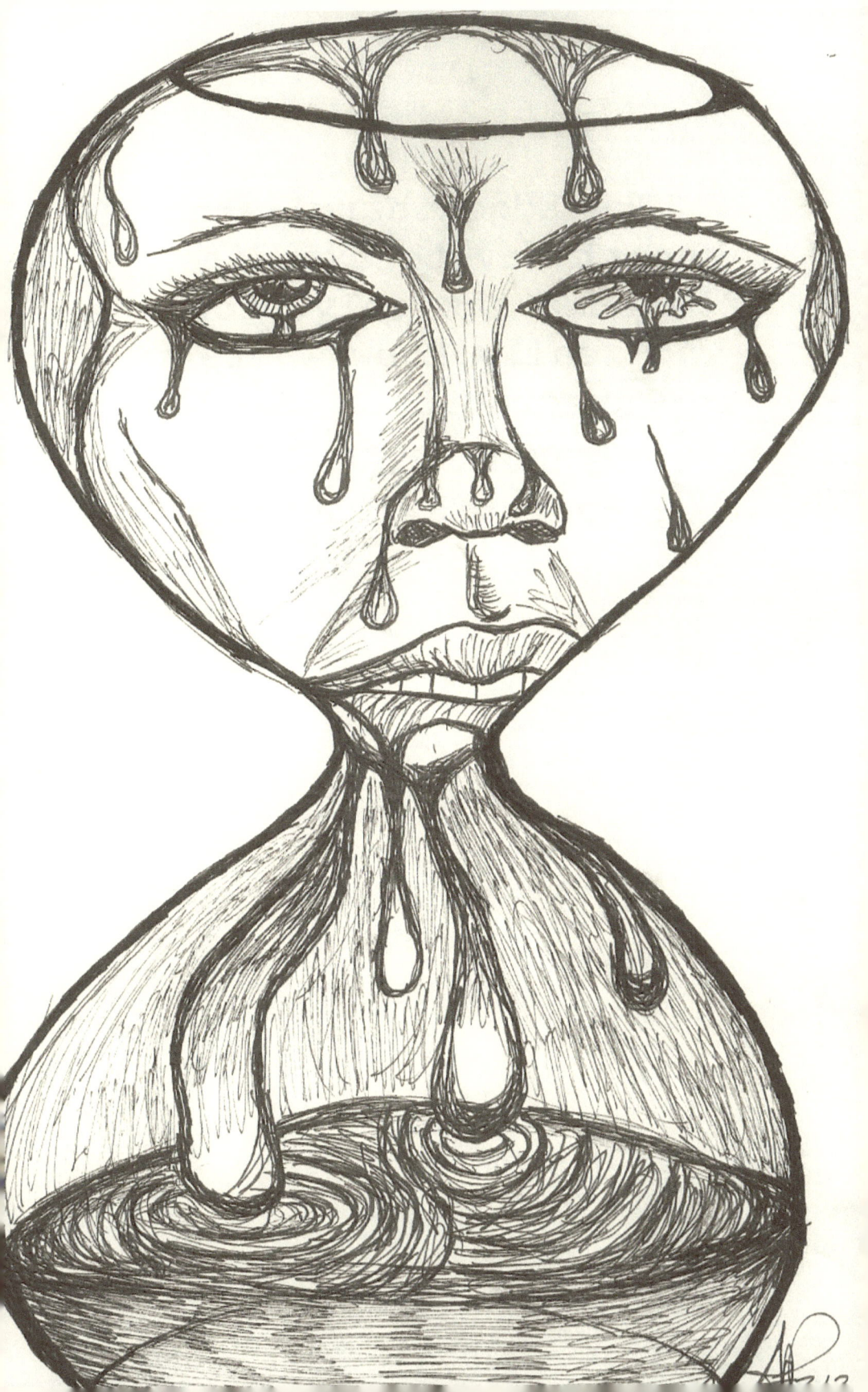

"The Edge...there is no honest way to explain it because the only people who really know where it is, are the ones who have gone over."

- Hunter S. Thompson

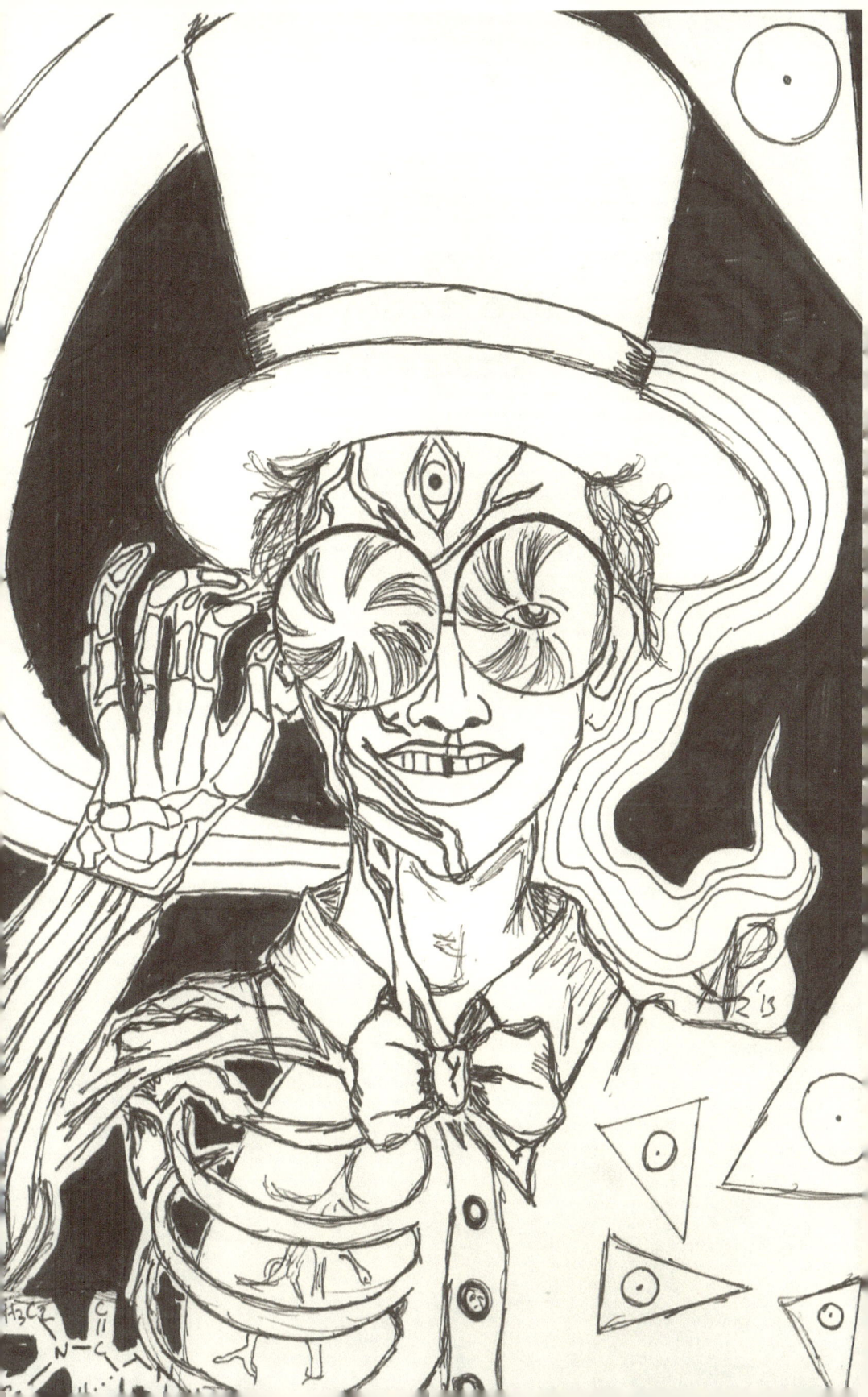

"Dream as if you'll live forever, Live as if you'll die today."

– James Dean

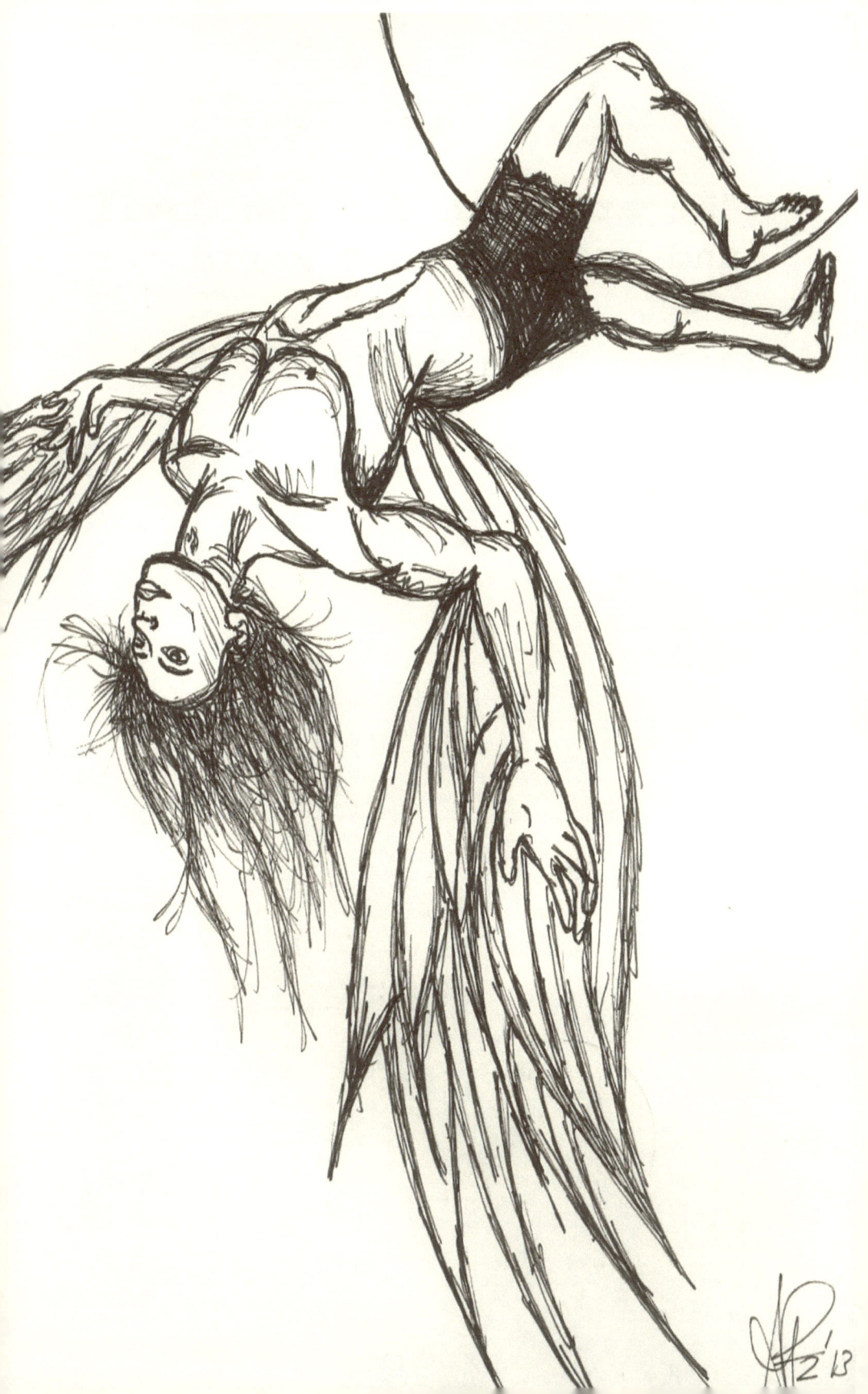

"We are each our own devil
and we make this world our
hell."

- Oscar Wilde

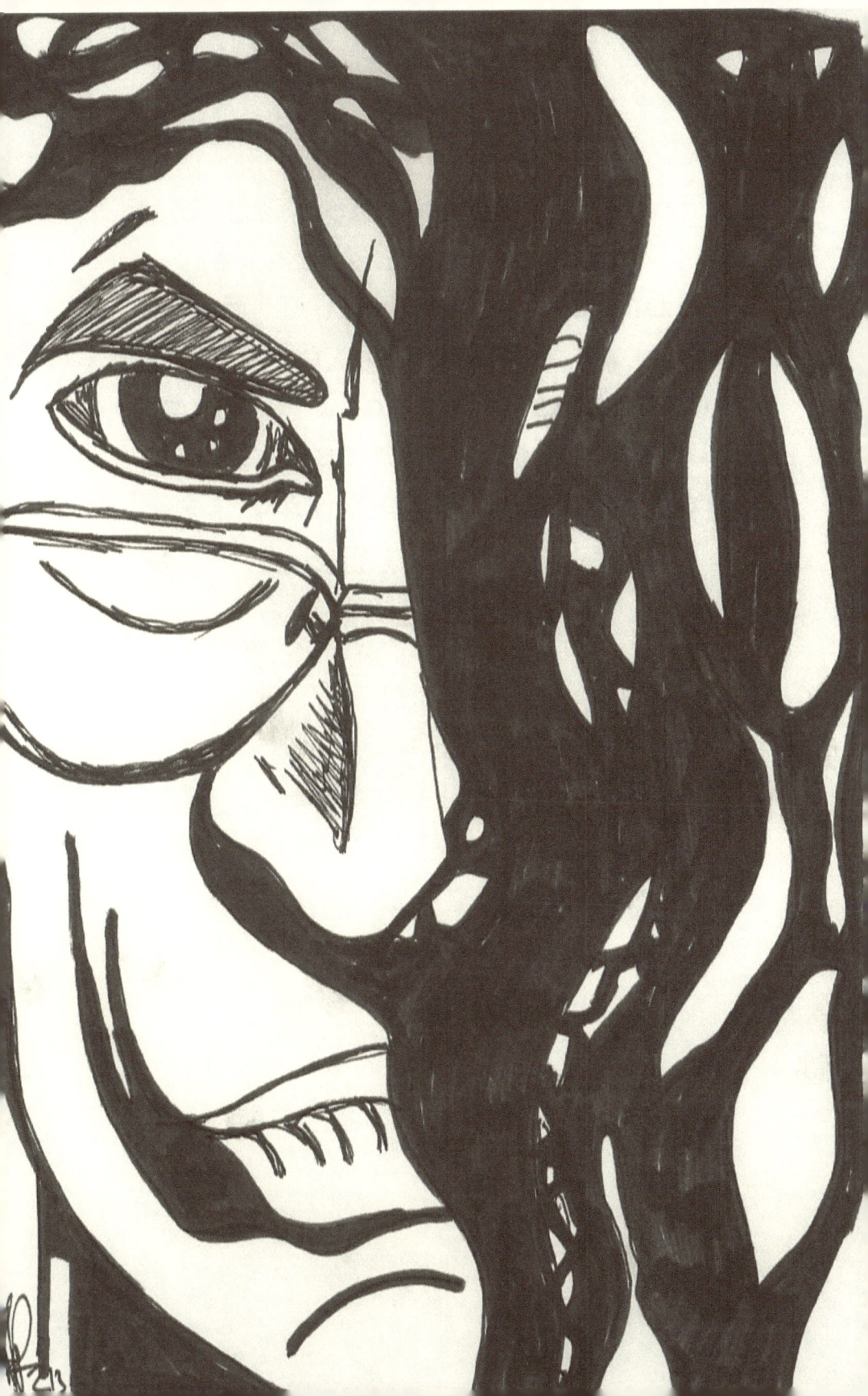

"You asked me how to get out of the finite dimensions when I feel like it. I certainly don't use logic when I do it. Logic's the first thing you have to get rid of."

\- J.D Salinger

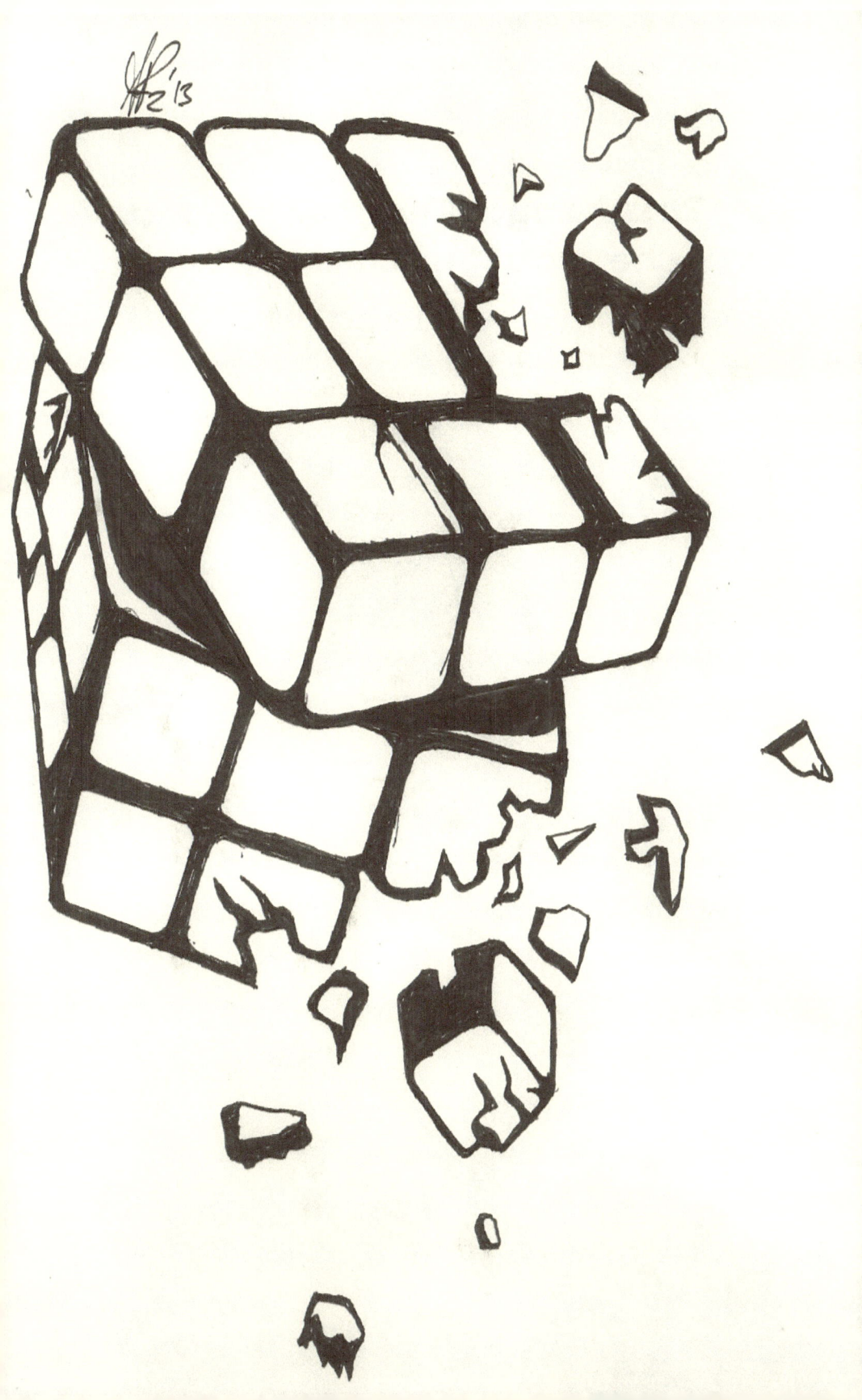

"Thinking: The talking of the soul with itself"

– Plato

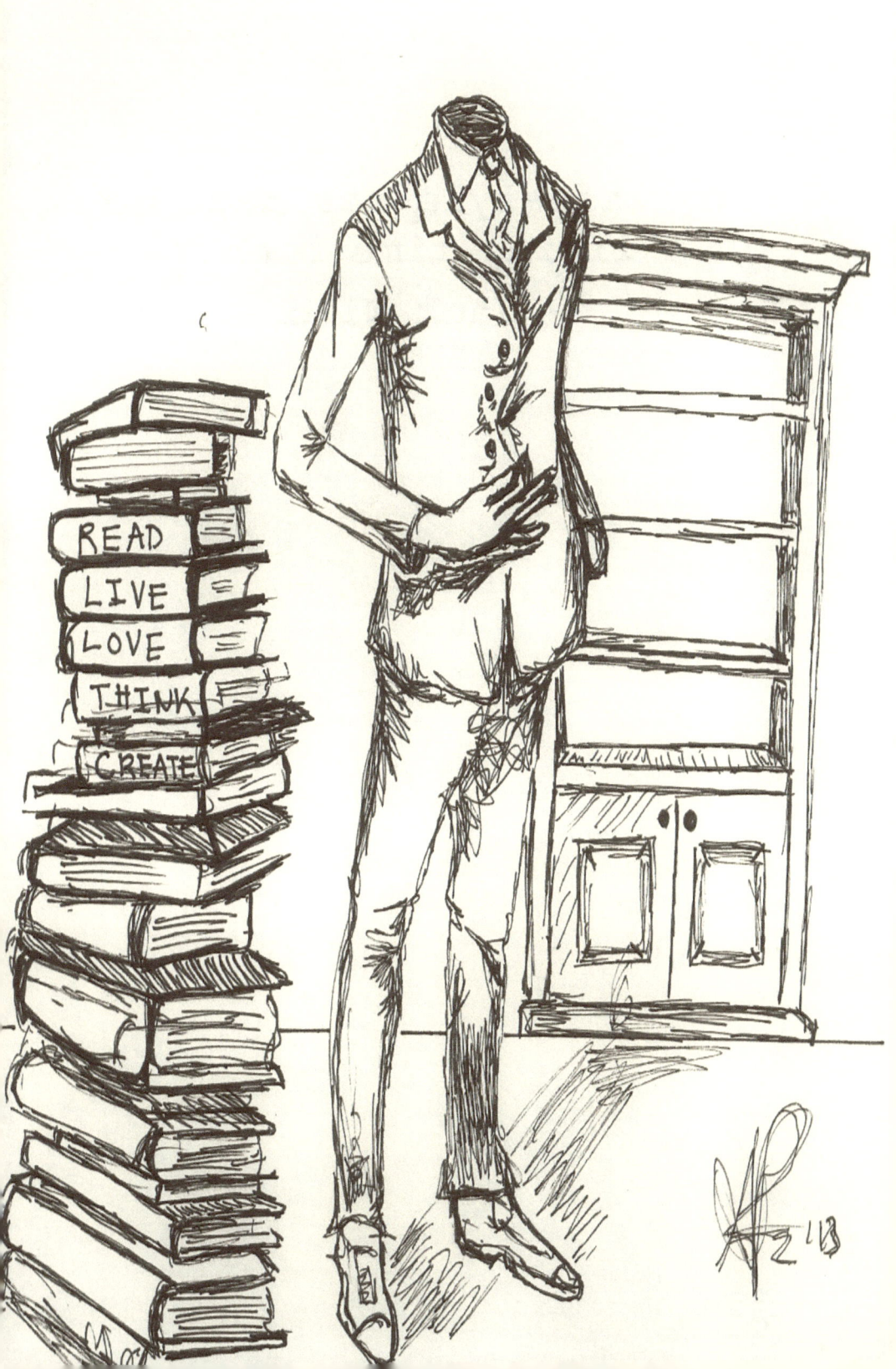

"My lifestyle has made me
a living time bomb."
- Jack Wild

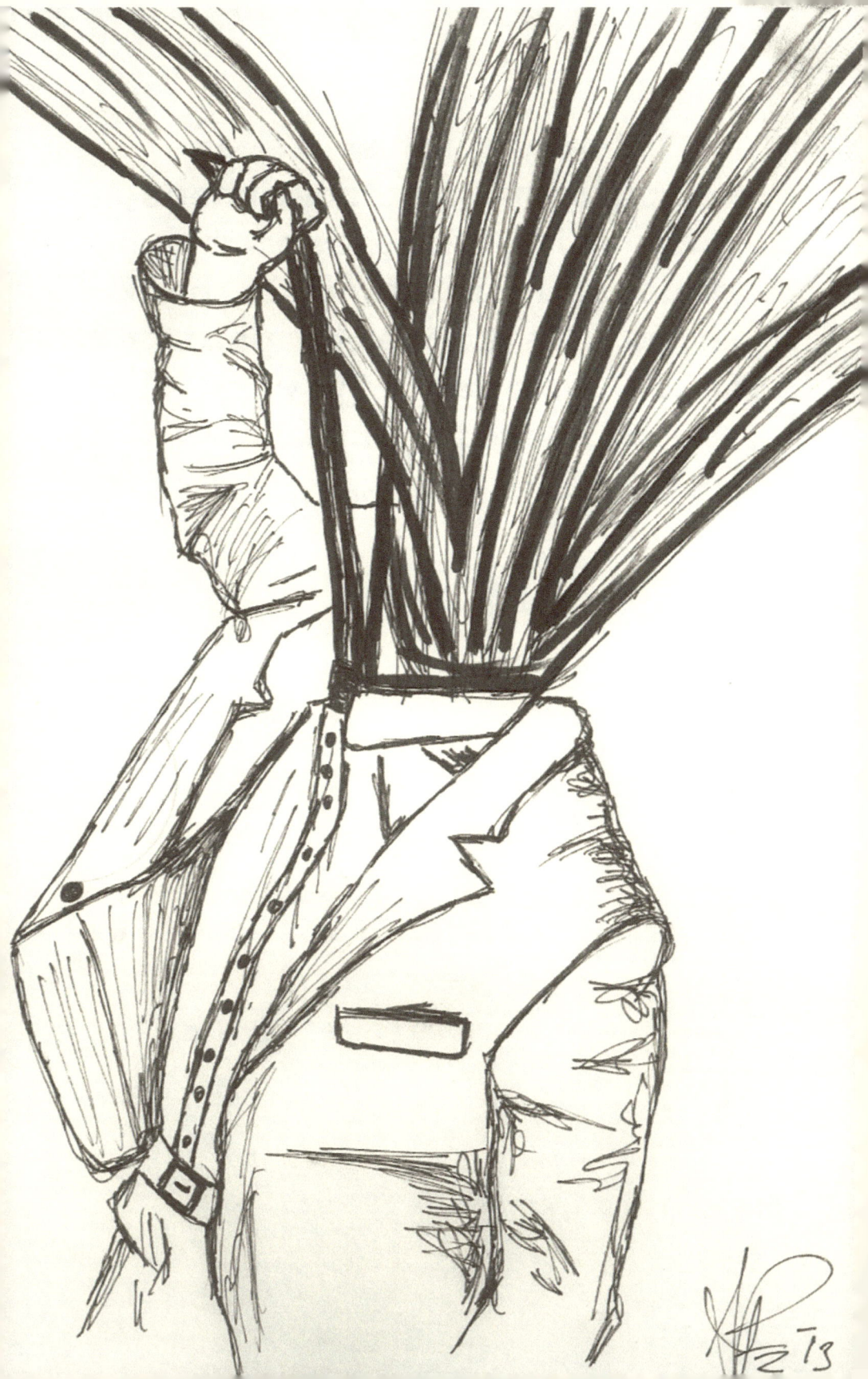

"Every smoker is an embodiment of Prometheus, stealing fire from the gods and bringing it back home. We smoke...to pacify hell, to identify with the primordial spark."

– Tom Robbins

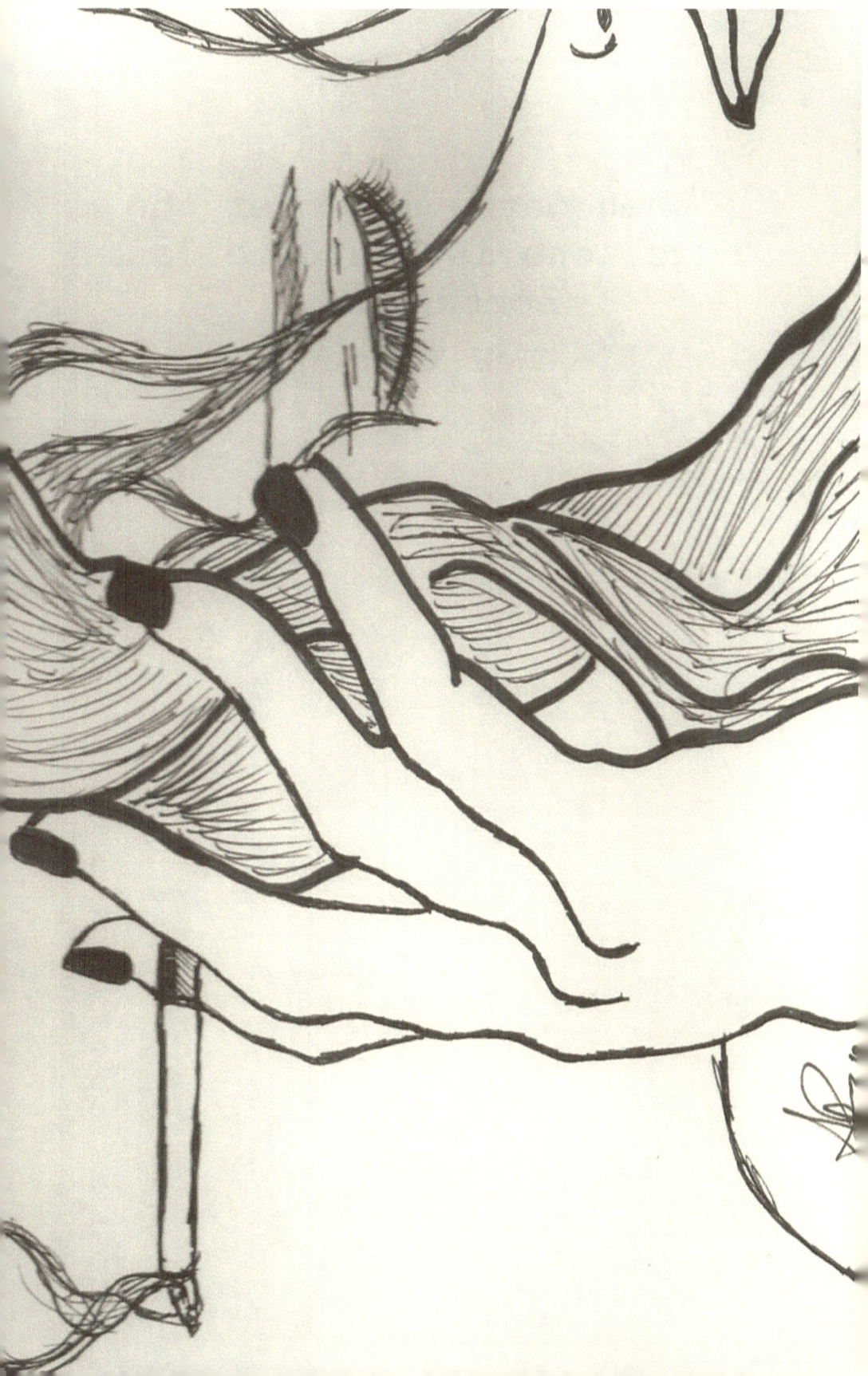

"When one jumps over the edge, one is bound to land somewhere."

- D.H Lawrence

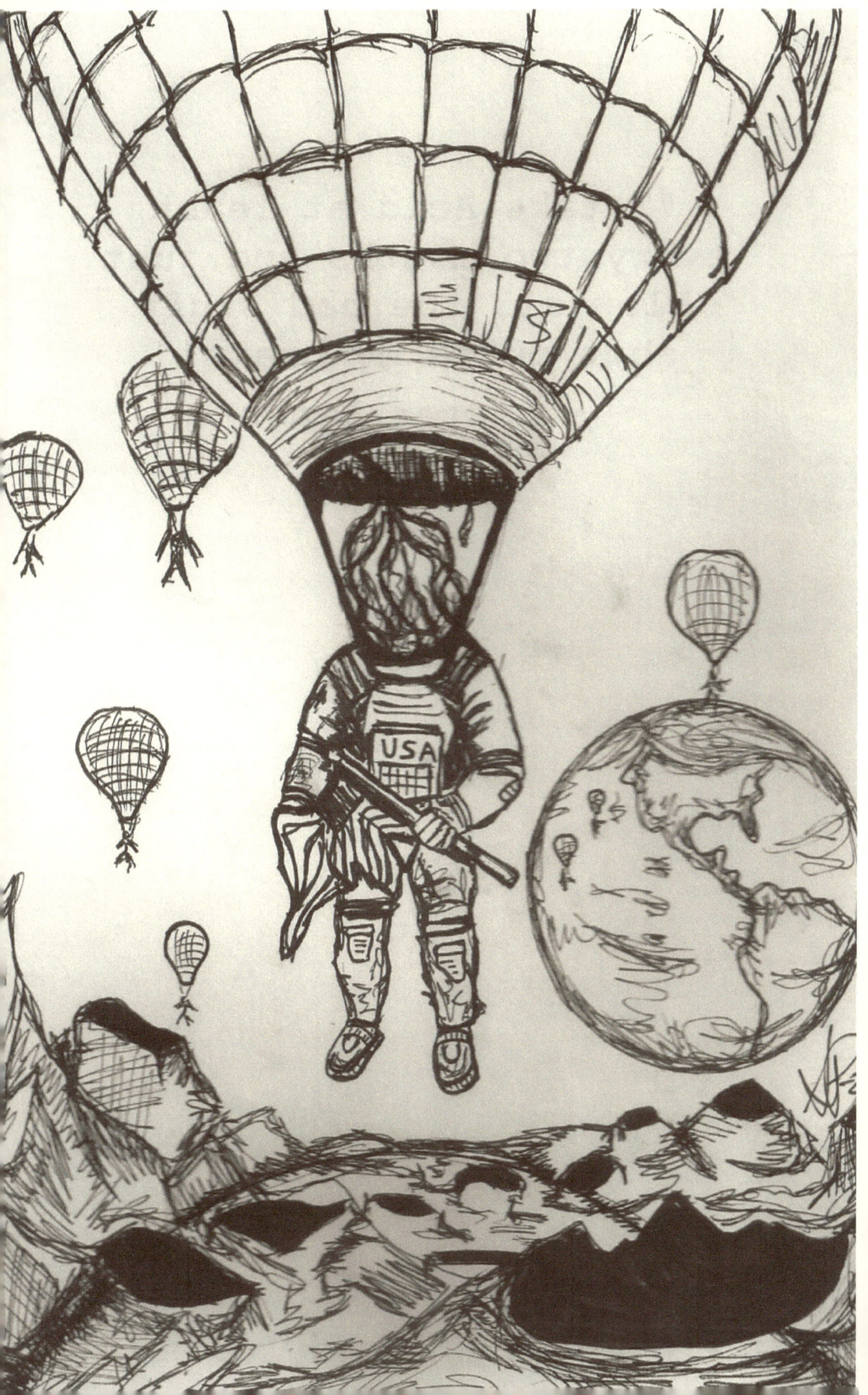

"I take Acid at least
every two months and just
blow all the bad stuff
shit outta my brain!"

- Lester Bangs

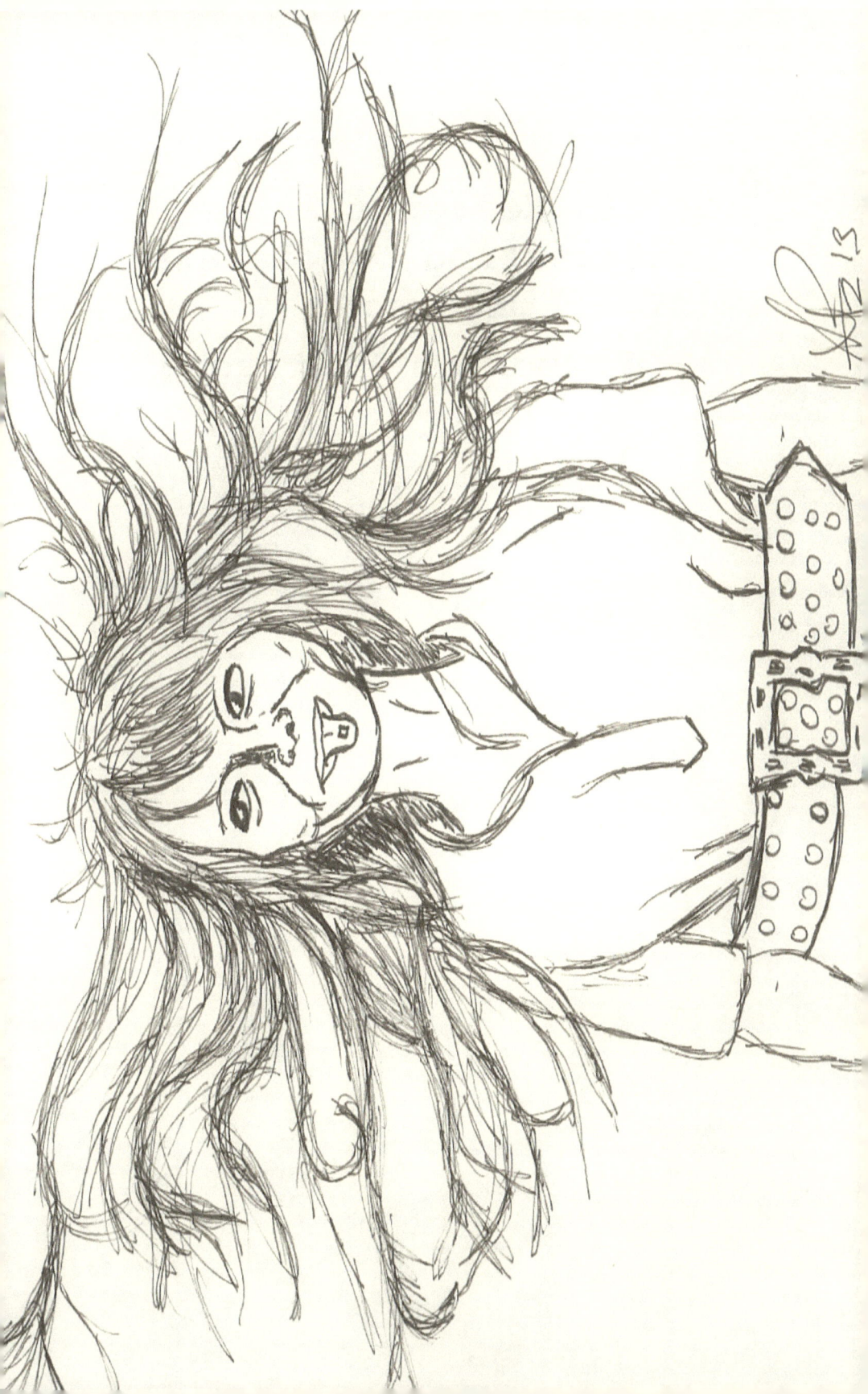

"In Heaven all the interesting people are missing."

- Friedrich Nietzsche

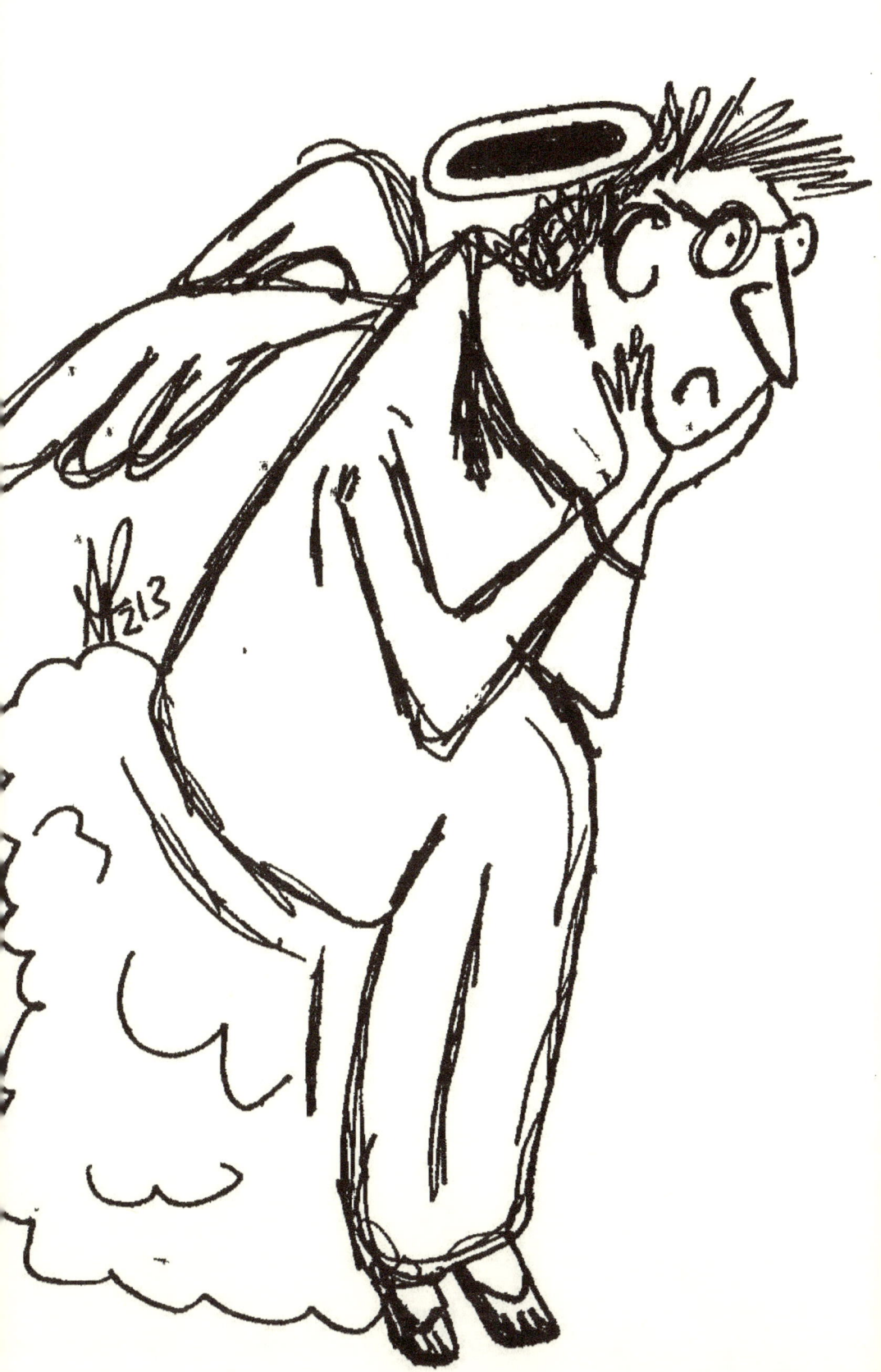

"We all need something to help us unwind at the end of the day. You might have a glass of wine, or a joint... to silence your silly brainbox of its witterings but there has to be some form of punctuation, or life just seems utterly relentless."
- Russell Brand

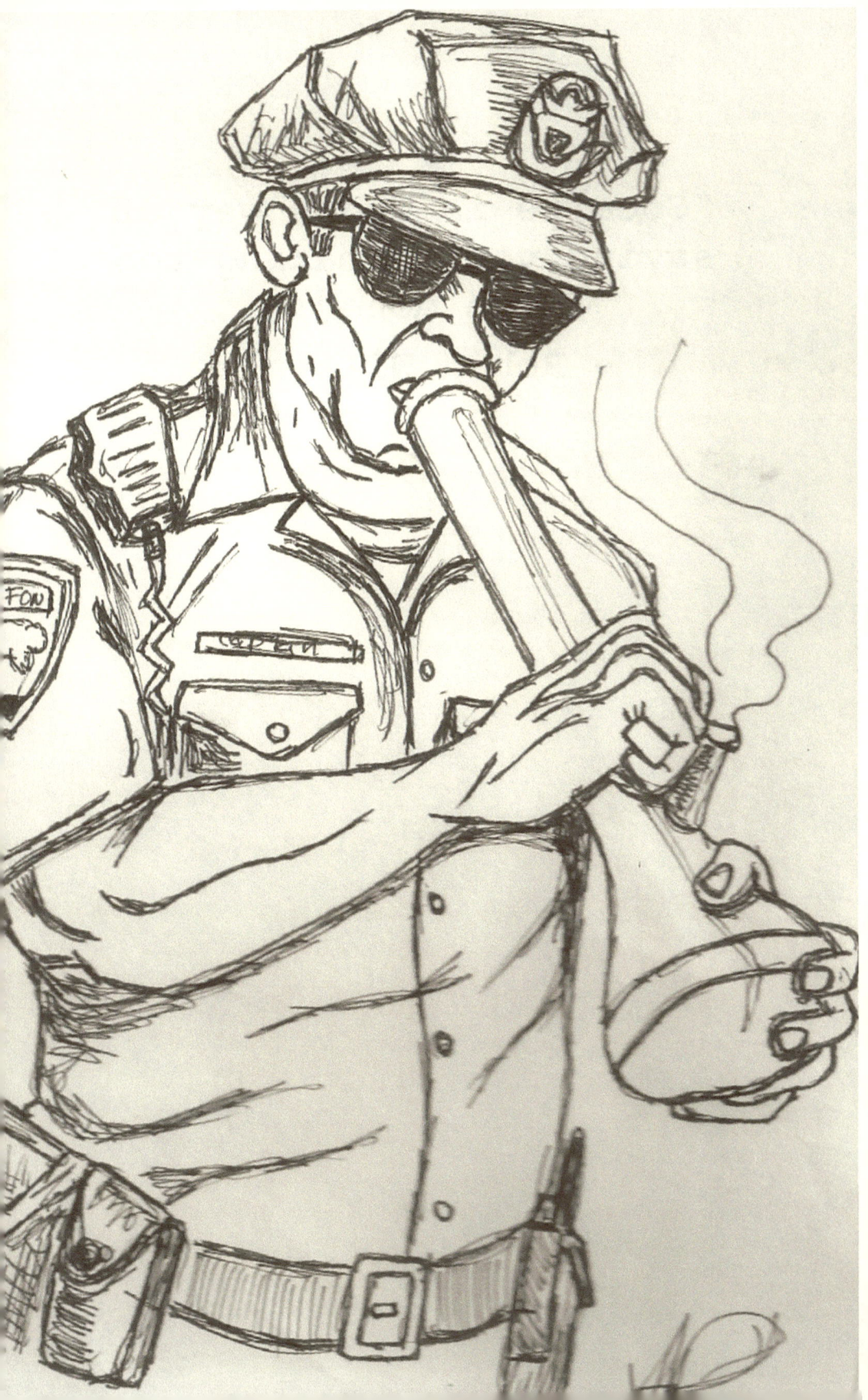

"Cocaine is God's way of saying you're making too much money."
- Robin Williams

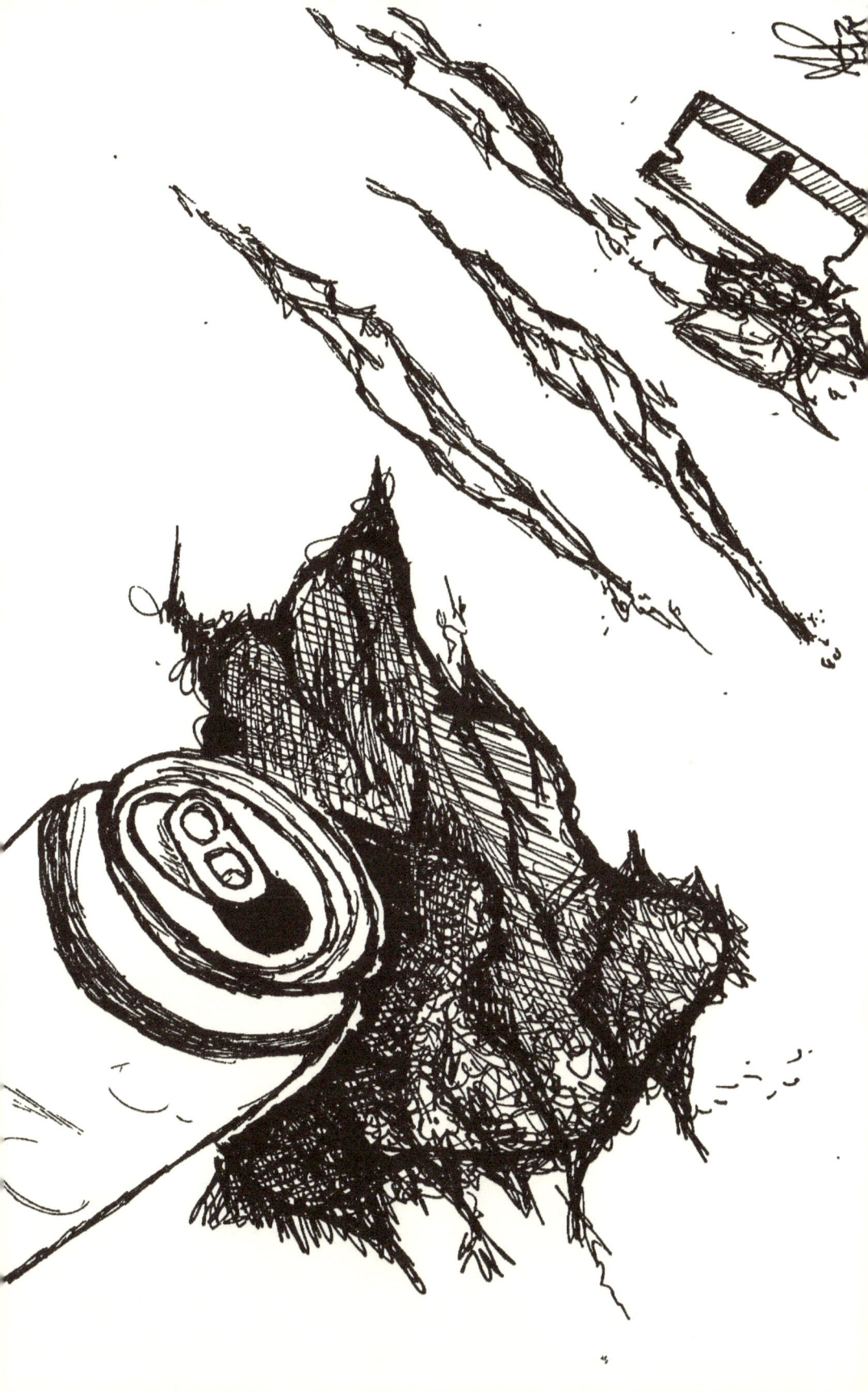

"America... just a nation of two hundred million used car salesmen with all the money we need to buy guns and no qualms about killing anybody else in the world who tries to make us uncomfortable."

– Hunter S. Thompson

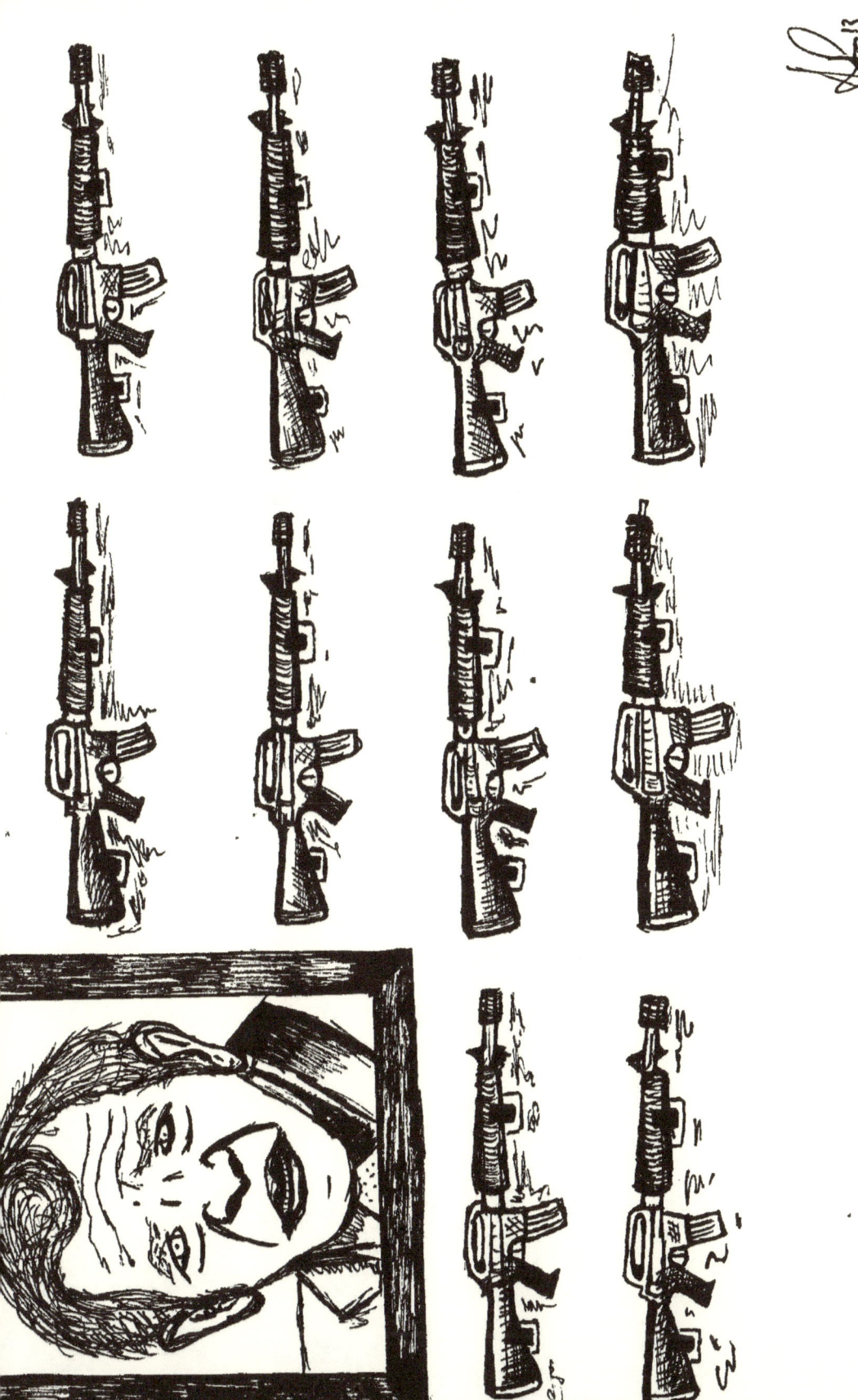

"Anyway, no drug, not even alcohol, causes the fundamental ills of society. If we're looking for the source of our troubles, we shouldn't test people for drugs, we should test them for stupidity, ignorance, greed and love of power."

-P. J. O'Rourke

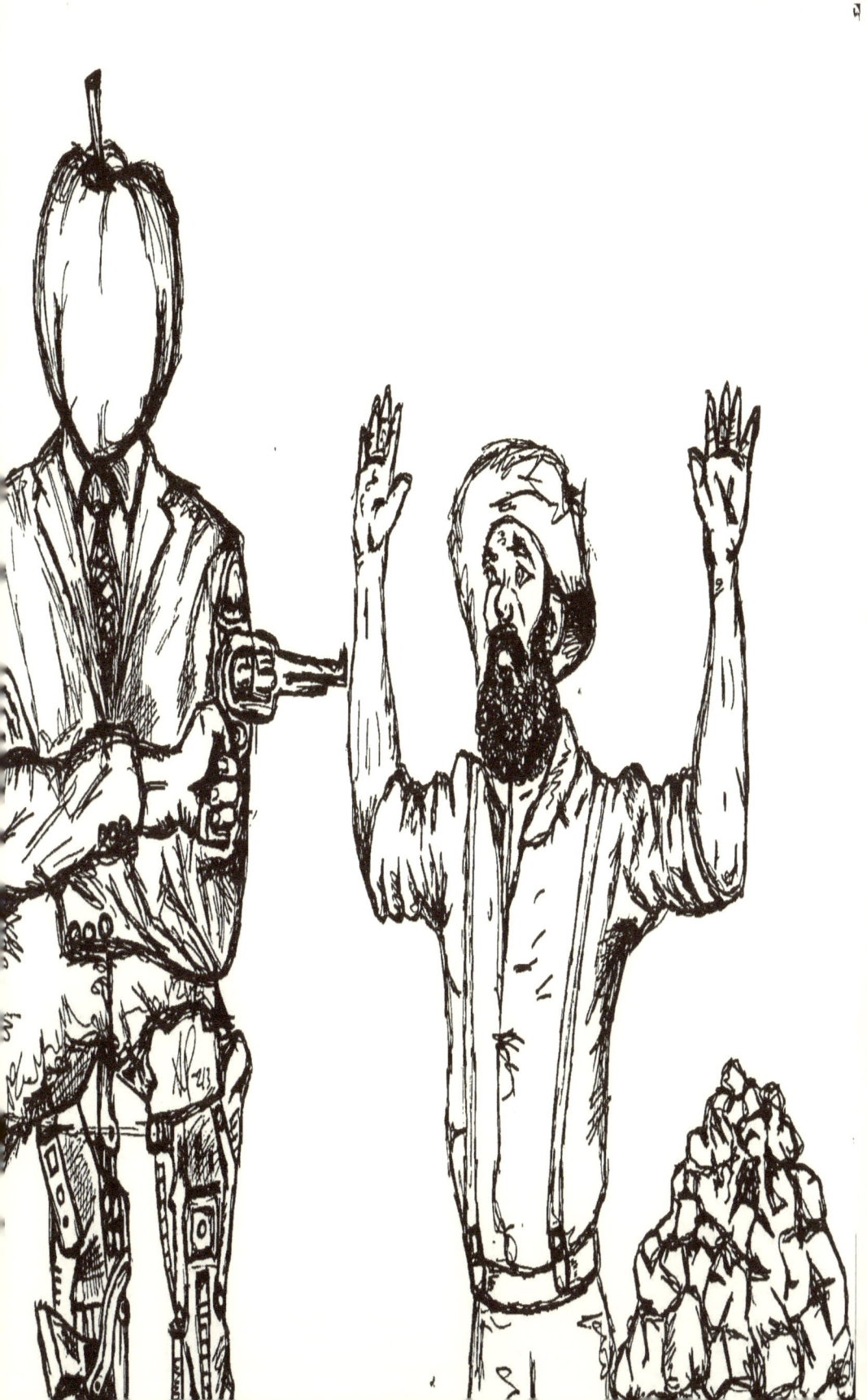

"I am enough of an artist to draw freely upon my imagination. Imagination is more important than knowledge. Knowledge is limited. Imagination encircles the world."

— Albert Einstein

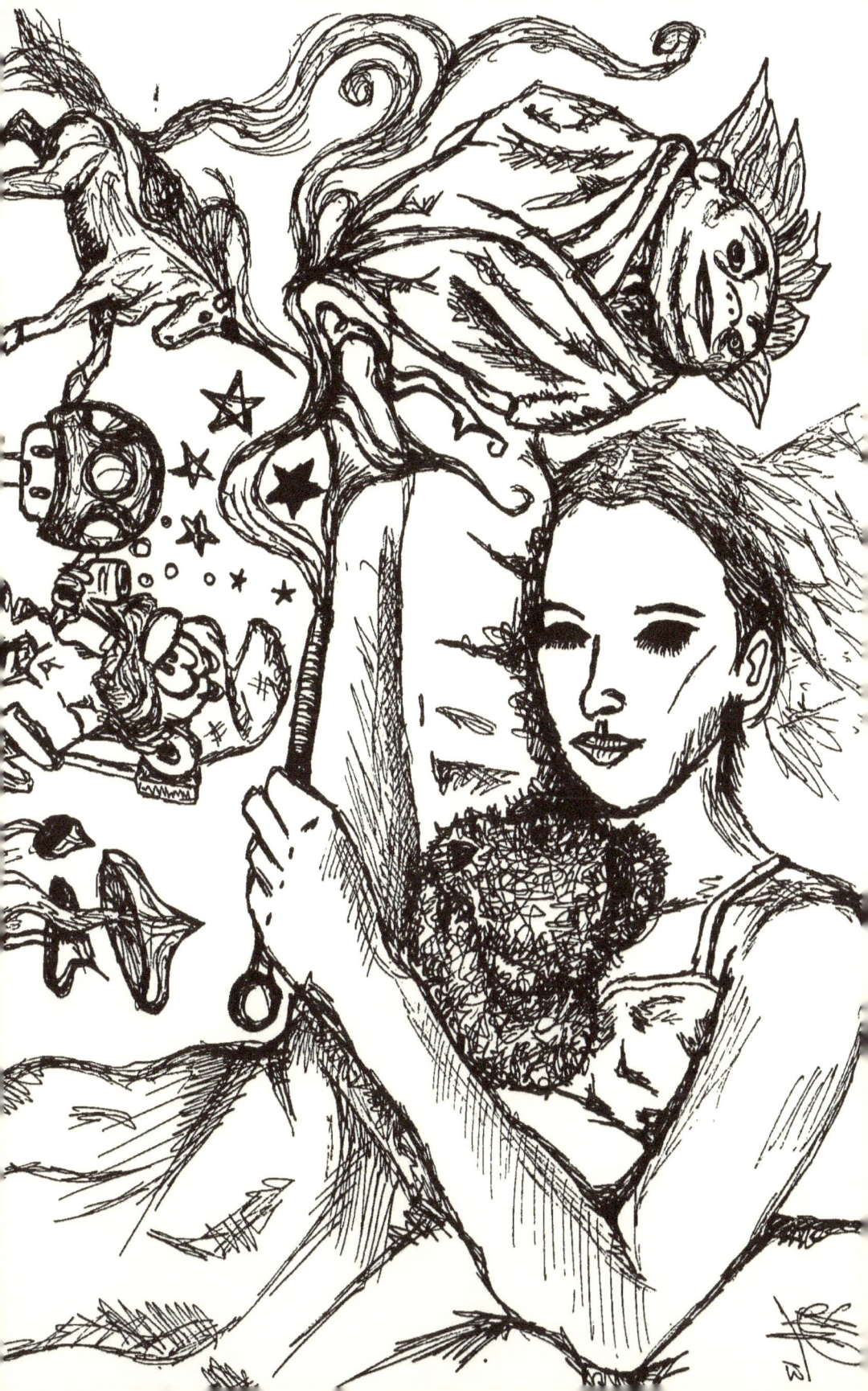

"Beauty is but skin deep, ugly lies the bone; beauty dies an fades away, but ugly holds its own"

- Albert Einstein

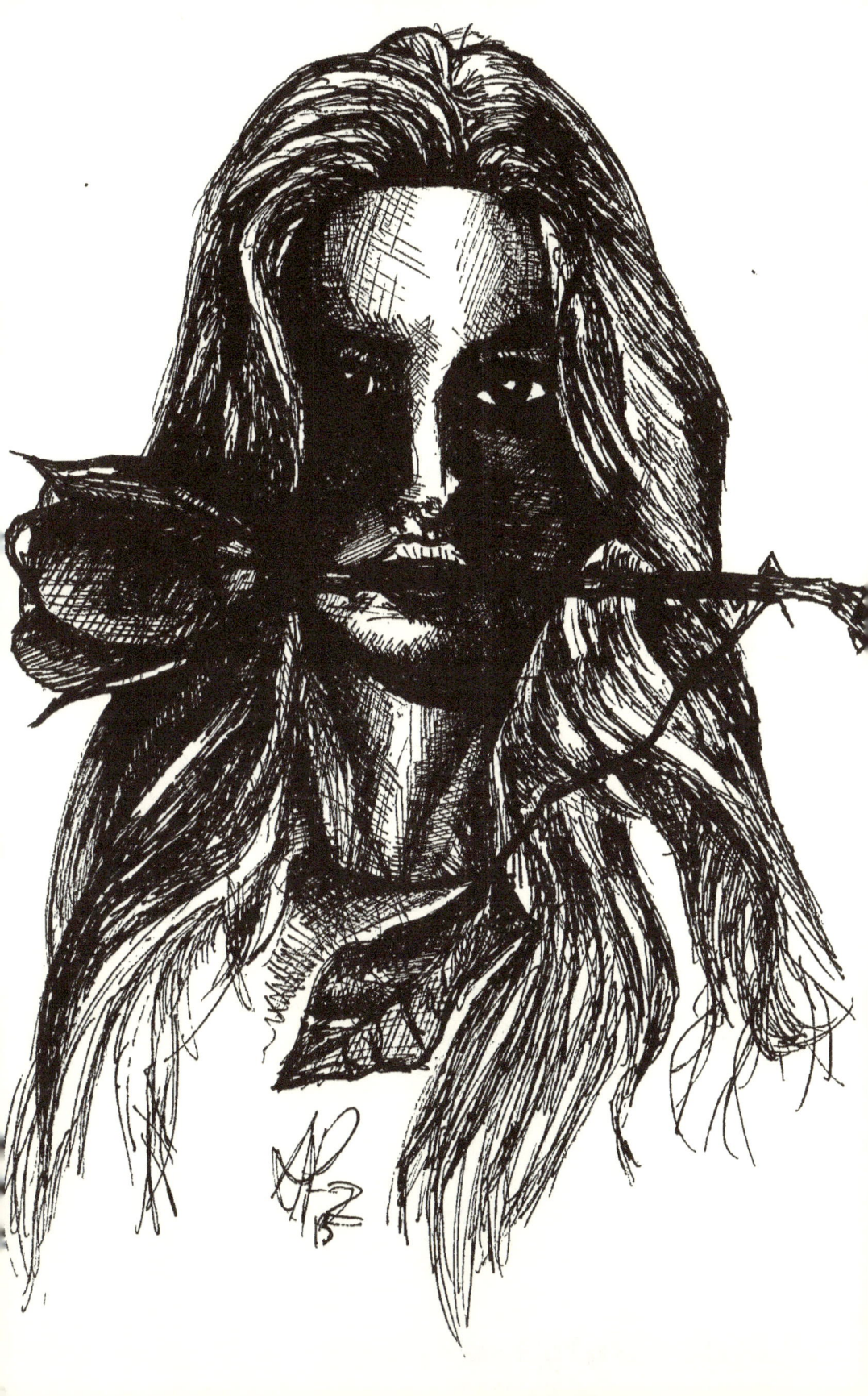

www.ingramcontent.com/pod-product-compliance
Lightning Source LLC
Chambersburg PA
CBHW021850170526
45157CB00006B/2381